Industrial Evolution 1750 to the present day

L. W. Cowie M.A., Ph.D. Lecturer in History, Whitelands College, Putney

D1740404

NELSON

1 The Old Way of Life

1. The industrial centres of England in 1750 (*map far right*, p. 3). Compare these scattered industries (in a mainly agricultural country) to Fig. 4.

2. These population figures for Manchester and Liverpool (*above*) and Glasgow, Birmingham and London (*far right*, p. 3) show the dramatic growth of some of Britain's leading towns.

3. The women of the family spin the wool in their cottage (*far right*).

For many centuries Britain was a very different land from the one we know to-day. Britain to-day has a population of nearly fifty-five million. Most of the people live in towns or cities, and some of these are very large indeed. The Greater London area has a population of eight million, Birmingham and Glasgow over a million each, while others, like Manchester or Sheffield, have about a half-million. Most of the people of Britain also work in factories, offices, or shops in occupations which are connected with industry and trade, with the making and selling of all sorts of articles from motor-cars to shoes, from tinned food to cigarettes. In other words, modern Britain is a thickly-populated country with a mainly urban, manufacturing people.

This, however, has only recently become so. Some two hundred years ago the people of Britain followed a way of life which had hardly changed for countless generations. Most of them lived in villages and small towns in the country side and were engaged in farming or rural crafts such as horse-shoeing, thatching, or carpentry. London was even then unique in its size. Its population had risen to about a half-million, but no other British town had as many as a hundred thousand inhabitants. Most towns were very small, situated some distance from each other and providing through their markets, fairs, and tradesmen for the needs of the countryside.

The few larger towns, which had a population of more than ten thousand each, were either ports like Bristol or Newcastle-upon-Tyne or important market towns like Exeter or Norwich. Such industries as existed were rural crafts. They were to be found in the countryside more commonly than in towns and were carried on in the homes of the workpeople themselves. The biggest industry in England at this time was the woollen industry which flourished chiefly in Yorkshire, East Anglia, and the West Country (see Fig. 1). The Lord Chancellor nowadays, when he presides over the meetings of the House of Lords, still sits on the woolsack, a large scarlet seat stuffed with wool as a reminder of what was once the greatest source of the nation's riches. English wool was reckoned to be among the best in the world, and wealthy merchants, known as clothiers, toured the countryside, buying it from the sheep-farmers. They took this wool to cottages where it first was spun into yarn and then woven into cloth. Often this might be done in the same cottages, the women doing the spinning and their husbands the weaving. Usually they owned their spinning-wheels and looms, though sometimes a clothier might supply them himself. When the cloth was finished, the clothier collected it from these workpeople, to whom he paid an agreed sum, and then sold it in England or abroad.

This method of organizing industry was known as the domestic system (Fig. 3), and most people who made things spent their days in this sort of way. The blacksmith lived beside his forge and the joiner over his workshop. Their work was part of their lives, and often their families helped them in it. They worked hard, sometimes exhaustingly hard, if they were to keep themselves and their families alive, but at the same time they enjoyed a great deal of freedom. They were on their own without anyone to supervize them or give them orders. They could often work in their own way and at their own speed. They were paid for what they made and knew that to a large extent their earnings depended upon their attitude towards their task.

For most men, their work had something else in common. It depended upon the power of their muscles. Only a few of them could use some other form of power to ease their labour. The miller relied upon wind to drive the sails which turned the great circular stones and ground the corn into flour; the iron-maker worked the bellows in his forge and the drop-hammer in his foundry through the force of running water; but the uses of wind and water power were limited. The carpenter at his bench, the weaver at his loom and nearly all other men had to exert unaided such strength as they had.

Ever since men had begun to make things, this way of doing it had been essentially the same. Men had mostly worked in their homes and depended upon their own natural strength. Then, during the eighteenth century, this manner of life began at last to change as the result of a momentous new movement.

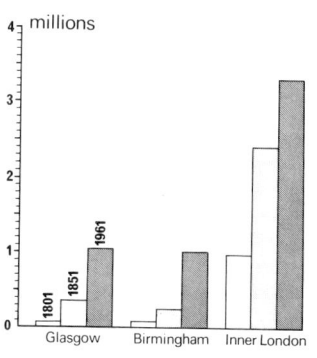

Background

1 What were the disadvantages of the domestic system? Look at Fig. 3. What sort of lighting would the cottages have had? Find out the working hours for typical domestic industries.

2 Do domestic systems still exist? Find out about carpet manufacture in Persia. Can you think of other examples of domestic industry? Are there still any in Britain?

3 Look at Fig. 7. Britain's industrial history is longer than any other country, yet Britain reached the later stages more slowly than the U.S.A. Why were other countries able to proceed more quickly than Britain?

2 The Industrial Revolution

The new movement which brought this change about is commonly called the Industrial Revolution. It was a tremendous, unprecedented change, though, as will be seen later in this book, it is now being followed by another equally important movement. Though it is called a 'revolution', it was not, of course, a revolution in the common sense of the word. Usually a revolution is a political happening, a rising by people against their rulers so that they may have a change of government. Such were the English Revolution of 1688 when James II was driven from the country or the French Revolution of 1789 when the monarchy of Louis XVI was replaced by a republic. The Industrial Revolution was not like these. It is true that it was sometimes accompanied by rioting and other violence, when unemployed men broke the machines which had deprived them of work, but these outbreaks sought vainly to halt the Industrial Revolution; they were not the events which brought it into being. It has been called a 'silent revolution', and yet it was more revolutionary in its results than any political revolution.

What the Industrial Revolution did was to break up the way of life which had lasted in Britain and other countries for more than fifteen hundred years. Within a short period of time the old rural, agricultural existence which people had followed for centuries was almost destroyed. A writer has recently expressed this in a striking way when he said that the manner of life of Jane Austen, the English novelist who lived from 1775 to 1819 in the Hampshire countryside, differs less from that of Homer, the great classical poet who lived about 850 B.C. in ancient Greece, than from ours today! Even a man who died only fifty years ago would hardly recognize many parts of Britain if he were able to come back and revisit them and see what had happened there since the days when he knew them. The changes brought about by the Industrial Revolution have not only been great and rapid, but have also continued to go on year by year until we are now being faced with another Industrial Revolution which is likely to be equally momentous in its consequences.

When did the Industrial Revolution begin? This is a question that, in a way, it is impossible to answer. We know that the French Revolution began when the mob stormed the Bastille, the massive royal prison-fortress in Paris, on 14 July 1789, but the Industrial Revolution has no definite date which may be said to mark its beginning. Instead historians have had to suggest a rough date which may be taken as about the time when it was beginning to take serious

4. England's industrial centres in 1850 (*right*). Compare this map to Fig. 1 and you can see how the pattern has changed and concentrated.

5. A view of Manchester across the River Irwell in 1745 (*far right*, p. 5) . . .

6. . . . and in 1969.

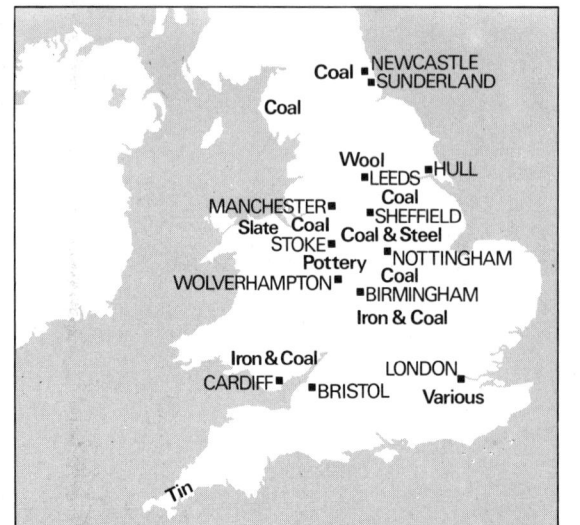

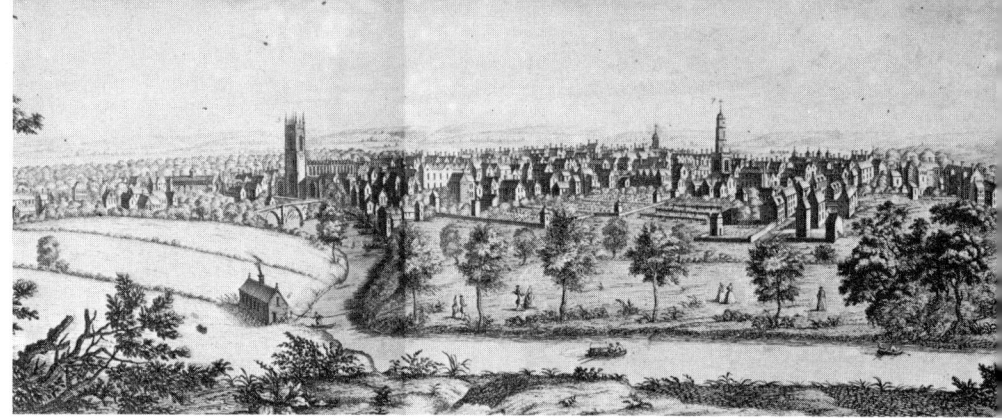

effect. The usual date given by historians has been 1760, but recently some have said that 1780 would be more accurate. At any rate, we may take it that the Industrial Revolution can be regarded as effectively beginning at some time in the second half of the eighteenth century, though there were earlier inventions and other developments which prepared the way for the changes of that period.

What was the nature of the Industrial Revolution? Essentially it may be said to have brought about two great alterations in the way men did their work. It replaced human muscle-power by machines which were driven by new forms of power – water and steam, electricity and petrol. It also replaced the domestic system by the factory system, which was not only a new way of organizing industry, but also brought a new way of life for very many people.

This Industrial Revolution began in Britain. It began some fifty years earlier in this country than it did anywhere else in the world, and for over a century Britain was the most important of any industrial nation. It must seem surprising that this movement, which has changed the face of the civilized world and the life of its people, should have had its origins in such a small country, but it was due to a number of circumstances which occurred at this time and combined to bring about such decisive results.

Background

1 Find out about the sorts of protests against machines that occurred during the Industrial Revolution. Why did men break the machines? Find examples in modern newspapers of protests against new machinery that costs men their jobs.

2 Look at Fig 8. When was Britain's population growing fastest compared to other countries? Discuss how and why population suddenly grows.

3 The Uniqueness of Britain

Some of the most important reasons why the Industrial Revolution began first in Britain were economic. The country had large coalfields, and these were near deposits of iron ore which could be mined easily. It also had a long and deeply-indented coastline, providing many excellent harbours where great ports could be built. Moreover, many of the inlets penetrated deeply into important parts of the country, and there were no high mountain barriers to prevent roads and railways being built into inland areas. These deep inlets and good harbours made the country's rivers useful for transport, and, further, they were not likely to be seriously flooded and were rarely frozen. In addition, it was fortunate that most of the longest English rivers flowed eastwards because this meant that their mouths faced the great river outlets of the Continent with which British ships traded.

There were also political and social reasons for Britain's early industrial growth. It was a peaceful, tolerant country; industry was not hampered by wars or revolutions; and it did not suffer as in France, where the Huguenots, who were skilled craftsmen, were driven from the country in the seventeenth century because they were Protestants. It had an island position and built a strong navy which protected it from invasion and obtained overseas colonies. Unlike other European countries, the medieval guilds, which prevented a craftsman working outside his own town, were no more, and there were no internal customs barriers, which imposed heavy duties on goods going from one part of the country to another. British farm-workers were not serfs, bound to work on the land, but could go into the towns and get new jobs in factories, so that industry was not short of labour. Similarly, the British nobilty was not a closed caste. Wealthy men could gain titles and enter the House of Lords, and the wish to do this encouraged industrialists to work hard and become rich. Other people were ready to lend them the money they needed to begin their enterprises, and so was the Bank of England, which had been founded in 1694.

Again, events in British history encouraged the development of industry. Throughout the eighteenth century Britain fought a series of wars against her chief rival, France. These wars demanded guns, ammunition, ships and all sorts of supplies which industry had to make for the government. And largely as a result of these wars, Britain gained overseas colonies and began to trade with many parts of the world. This trade required an increasing variety of manufactured goods and also brought British industry the cotton and other raw materials it needed. At the same time, this trade made the country wealthier. People could afford to buy more things, and industry grew still more by making these for them.

Of course, there were other European countries at this time where some of these economic and other circumstances were present, but the important thing was that in Britain alone did they all combine to produce such outstanding consequences. For instance, until very late in the eighteenth century it seems that some of the large French industries, especially the iron and cotton industries, had a greater output than their British rivals. This, indeed, might be expected since the population of France was then three or four times the size of that of Britain;

7. The economic growth of twelve nations in all parts of the world (*far right*, p. 7). Find out what 'high mass-consumption' means. Why do you think that Canada has reached this stage before Britain, and before its industry was as highly developed as Britain's? Compare other countries in this way.

8. Population Change 1800–1970 (*far right*, p. 7).

but these French industries could not grow in a country where the manufacturers still had to obey the guild regulations which restricted changes and improvements, and where people with money preferred to invest it in safe government loans rather than risk it in trade or industry. British industry could thus accumulate capital in its early days on a larger scale than in France. Consequently Britain was able to overtake France and establish an absolute supremacy in industrialization.

Another factor which assisted the development of the Industrial Revolution in Britain was the rapid growth of her population (see Fig. 8). In 1760 she had only about eight million people, while France had perhaps nearly twenty-five million; but by the end of the nineteenth century Britain's population had increased five-fold and overtaken that of France, which would have been unbelievable at one time. A steadily multiplying population meant that there was always a new labour force for the new industries. It also meant that Britain had a large home market for her manufactured products which provided a healthy basis for her export trade.

Revolutions are usually the result of the actions of a few thinkers and leaders, and this was true of the Industrial Revolution in Britain. First there were a handful of scientists like Sir Isaac Newton (the expounder of the laws of gravity) or Joseph Priestly (the discoverer of oxygen), whose efforts were of important practical application in industry. Then there were the inventors and manufacturers, also comparatively few in number, whose achievements make up the story of the Industrial Revolution.

Background
1 Find out what sort of immigrants came to Britain before the present century. What sort of skills did they bring and where did they live?

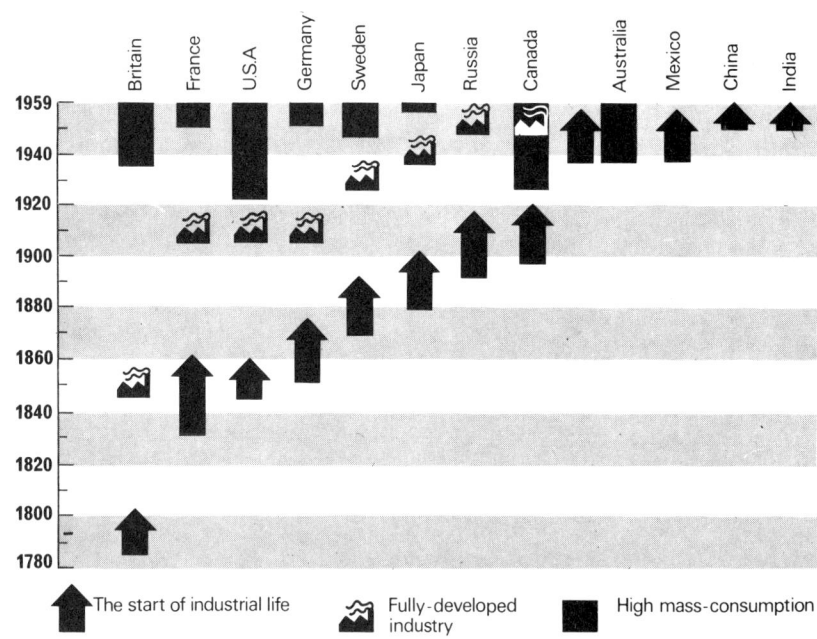

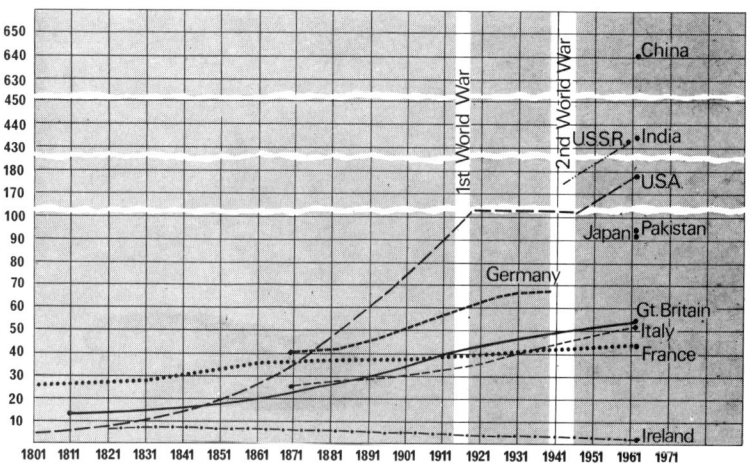

4 Discoveries and Inventions

Some historians have said that the first signs of the Industrial Revolution in Britain came when men began to smelt iron with coke. The iron industry had existed in Britain since long before the Roman occupation, and at the beginning of the eighteenth century it was dispersed in a number of areas, East Sussex being an important one and the Forest of Dean in Gloucestershire being another. The industry had to be established not only near to iron ore, but also to forests and running water. Wood was needed because charcoal was used for smelting, that is heating the ore in blast-furnaces to rid it of impurities, while the bellows of the blast-furnaces and the trip-hammers of the forges (in which the iron was shaped) were worked by water power. Consequently ironworks were situated along the banks of rivers and surrounded by woodland; but centuries of charcoal-making had destroyed many forests, and the ironworks were facing an uncertain future. Attempts had been made to use coal for smelting, but its sulphurous fumes made the iron impure and brittle. Fortunately, Abraham Darby and his son, who had an ironworks at Coalbrookdale in Shropshire (see Fig. 12), made a series of discoveries between 1709 and 1750 which rendered it possible to produce good iron by smelting the ore with coke.

This saved the iron industry, which could

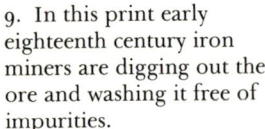

9. In this print early eighteenth century iron miners are digging out the ore and washing it free of impurities.

now increase its output enormously and no longer had to be scattered among woods and along rivers. It gradually concentrated itself among the coalfields of the North and Midlands, South Wales and the Scottish Lowlands. The new coke-operated blast-furnaces, however, still made pig-iron, so-called because it ran from the furnace to harden in shallow ditches called pigs, and this was not strong enough for many purposes. Wrought-iron was stronger, but this was made by heating the iron again with charcoal and hammering it in the forge to remove all the impurities, which was a long and costly process. The problem was solved by Henry Cort, who in 1794 invented a reverberatory furnace in which the ore was heated and stirred to produce wrought-iron fifteen times as quickly as before. He also invented grooved rollers to change large ingots of wrought-iron quickly and cheaply into usable bars and sheets.

Now the British iron industry was well able to meet the needs of the Industrial Revolution. The new age which was now coming into being has sometimes been called the 'machine age', but since machines could not be made without iron, it might perhaps be more accurate to call it the 'iron age'. And this new iron age was also the 'coal age' because as the iron industry steadily grew it increasingly demanded coal. Mine shafts had to be dug deeper and galleries made longer to get more coal. This brought yet more problems. One was the threat of flooding, the solution of which was to be bound up very closely with the development of steam power. Another was the danger from fire-damp, the explosive gas so often found in underground workings. This was overcome in 1815 when Sir

10. Wood, coated with clay, is stacked in a pyramid and burnt to produce the charcoal.

Humphrey Davy invented a safety-lamp (Fig. 13), in which the flame was enclosed in a cylinder of fine wire-gauze through which it could not pass and would not, therefore, ignite the fire-damp.

Though the iron and coal industries made rapid progress in the eighteenth century, the greatest English industry – next to farming, which continued throughout the century to employ more people than any other occupation – was the textile industry, which produced woollen and cotton cloth. Both were important, but the cotton industry grew much more rapidly in size both because fashionable English ladies wanted light dresses of calico and muslin and because cotton goods found a ready sale in overseas tropical markets. Its expansion was hindered, however, by the slowness of the old ways of spinning and weaving. Now the development of the iron industry made it possible to introduce new devices and machines to over-

11. The iron founders' workshop, from a print of 1803 (*above*).

12. The ironworks at Coalbrookdale in 1788 (*right*). Notice the riverside site and the waterwheel.

10

come this disadvantage. The first important invention of this sort was the fly-shuttle devised by John Kay in 1733. This enabled a weaver to jerk the shuttle across the loom and back again using one hand only. The speed of weaving was doubled, and a single weaver could make cloths of any widths. Previously two men had sat together at a loom to make broad cloths. It was followed in 1764 by the spinning-jenny, invented by James Hargreaves, which similarly speeded-up the process of spinning the thread and was so simple that a child could operate it.

Background

1 Find out what was the first industry in your own area. On a map of the area mark in buildings that still exist. How was your area affected by the new inventions?

2 What garments were made of cotton in the eighteenth and nineteenth centuries? Compare the types of garments to modern uses of cotton.

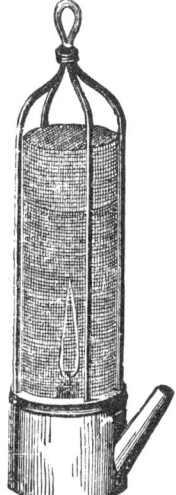

Fig. 576. THE DAVY.

It was to guard against the explosion of fire-damp, that Sir Humphry Davy invented his safety lamp, Fig. 576, a beautiful and simple contrivance, consisting merely of a common oil lamp, the flame of which is completely enclosed within a cylinder of wire gauze, which, as already explained in our article CANDLE, will not admit of the passage of flame; so that although the lamp be introduced into an explosive mixture, the flame will not pass through the gauze to ignite it. Of course, the efficacy of the lamp depends on the soundness of the wire gauze, for if this be broken and injured, the flame is not protected; or if the lamp be moved swiftly through an explosive atmosphere, the flame may be blown against, and even through the meshes of the gauze, and, in either case, might lead to an explosion.

13. A contemporary description of the Davy Lamp (*left*).

14. Coalbrookdale (Fig. 12) had its own coal mine, and this print (*left*) shows the mouth of the shaft. The great wheel, worked by horses, raised and lowered the men to the coal face in a bucket. Carts on tracks were forerunners of the railways.

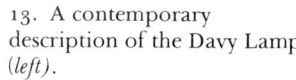

5 New Forms of Power

The fly-shuttle and the spinning-jenny were both devices which improved the way in which weaving and spinning could be performed, but, like the old loom and the spinning-wheel which they replaced, they were still hand-operated. They relied upon human skill and strength to achieve their purpose. The next stage in the development of the textile industry was to use other forms of power. The first to be put into use was one of the oldest known to men – water power. In 1769 Richard Arkwright invented the water-frame, a spinning-frame worked by water power, which spun a stronger thread than had ever been possible before, but could not produce fine thread, which still had to be hand-spun. In 1779, however, Samuel Crompton combined the spinning-jenny and the water-frame in his spinning-mule which could produce the fine materials demanded by ladies. These power-driven spinning-machines produced thread quickly, but weaving remained slow on the hand-looms until in 1785

15. Hargreave's spinning jenny, 1764.

a Leicestershire clergyman, Edmund Cartwright, invented a power-loom.

Water-power alone, however, would not have made the Industrial Revolution possible. Steam power was the great driving force which enabled the movement to take place. It was the need to pump water out of the mines which led to the invention of the steam-engine. The first effective steam-engine was made by Thomas Newcomen in 1708 (Fig. 16). It was a large, stationary engine above the boiler of which was an upright cylinder open at the top, and in this the piston was forced up by steam admitted at the base; then cold water was let into the cylinder which condensed the steam and created a vacuum to make the piston fall. The piston was attached to a pivoted beam, the other end of which was attached to a pump.

Newcomen's engine, however, had three serious defects. It wasted fuel because the cylinder was alternately heated by the injection of steam and cooled with cold water to create a vacuum; it was limited to an up-and-down motion; and it used steam pressure to drive the piston only in one direction. These defects were all remedied by James Watt. In 1765 he fitted a separate condenser so that the cylinder was no longer continually cooled and reheated; and he went on in 1782 to make it into a double-acting engine in which steam was admitted alternately on each side of the piston and to fit a crank-shaft and cog-wheel to the piston which gave it a rotary instead of an up-and-down movement.

The steam-engine now was much more powerful then before and could drive machinery. For the first time in his history man had a source of power which would effectively replace his own

muscles. Watt co-operated with an iron-maker, Matthew Boulton, to manufacture the new engines at Birmingham, and by 1800 some five hundred of them were at work in Britain, driving the spinning-machines and looms in textile mills, working hammers and cranes, blowing the bellows in blast-furnaces, operating mechanical presses and moulds and performing numerous other tasks in industry. After James Boswell, the friend of Dr Johnson, had visited the Birmingham engine-works, he wrote, 'I shall never forget Mr Boulton's expression to me, "I sell here, sir, what all the world desires to have – power"'.

The Industrial Revolution depended at first almost completely on steam power, but as it progressed other forms of power were discovered. A serious rival to the steam-engine first appeared in the 1870s when the electric motor was invented, and gradually electricity was used instead of steam-power in many industries because it was cheaper, quieter and cleaner.

And in our own century the discovery of atomic power is equally revolutionary. Atomic energy can provide heat which produces steam to make electricity. The electric generators are driven by steam-turbine engines, invented by Sir Charles Parsons in 1884, in which the steam turns the blades of a wheel, achieving greater power and speed than the older piston-driven steam-engines. The first nuclear power station was built in Britain in 1956 at Calder Hall in Cumberland, and an increasing amount of the electricity used in Britain will come from such stations.

16. Newcomen's steam engine, 1708 (*below left*).

17. As with every new invention, some people felt that steam was a step in the wrong direction. In this cartoon (*below*) George Cruikshank imagined steam driven carriages and even men, and called the result 'A few small inconveniences'.

Background
1 Make a list of the uses of steam and put beside each one the new source of power that has replaced it. Are there any jobs for which steam power is still used?
2 Look at Fig. 37. Find out the uses of the various buildings shown. What is the raw material used in nuclear power stations? Where does it come from?

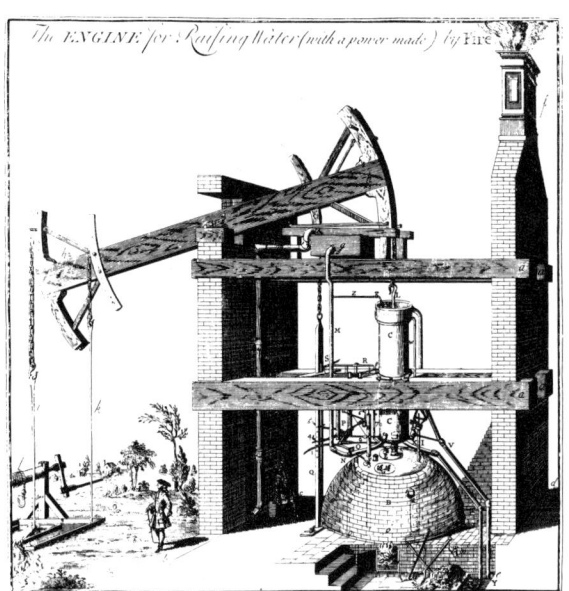

6 The Factory System

The old domestic system was not suited to industry once machinery and the new forms of power were introduced. It had worked all right in the days when production had been on a small scale and by hand; but now the workers had to leave their homes and come together in one place to work the machines engaged in the various processes of manufacture, all of which were operated by means of gear-wheels or belts from an axle moved by a single water-wheel or steam-engine. So there came into being the factories which soon became a familiar part of the industrial landscape of Britain.

As the cotton industry grew more rapidly than any other, the most numerous factories at first were the cotton-mills. The earliest mills, which relied on water-power, were built by streams in the Pennine hills or the Lancashire moors. Later, when steam-engines were used to drive the machinery, they were built in towns near the coalfields. This change was unfortunate for the mill-workers. Those who had lived in small villages in the hills or the moors were still country-dwellers, but the great towns which grew up around the later mills were crowded and ill-planned. Their houses were small and badly-built. Many were without water or drainage. The streets were filthy and unlit. Smoke and dirt were everywhere. In such surroundings disease was common, and few people lived to old age.

Nor was that all. When people came from the country to go into the factories, they found that conditions were very different from those they had known when they had worked in their cottages or on the land. The old freedom they had known was gone. The mill-owners imposed a strict system of discipline. Wages were low, holidays were few, and hours were long. In Manchester in 1818 the working-hours were from five in the morning until eight or nine at night with only a single break for three-quarters of an hour at lunch-time. There were fines for lateness, talking at work or even opening a window. The machines were noisy, and the atmosphere of the mills was kept hot and moist to prevent the cotton threads snapping when stretched. No wonder that men used to the older way of life found it hard to submit to these conditions.

Because of this, mill-owners employed large numbers of women and children (Fig. 18), who were more docile and amenable to discipline. Moreover, their wages were less, and their nimble fingers and shorter stature enabled them to undertake delicate threading tasks among the machinery. Their hours of work were rarely shorter then those of the men, and they often had to move among fast-revolving, dangerous machinery. Discipline was imposed upon them by physical punishment. Overseers frequently kept both young women and children at their tasks with a strap or cane.

When these conditions became known, a number of reformers began to demand that Parliament should take action to protect work-people. The first two acts to be passed were in 1802 and 1819. These sought to limit the working-day of children under the age of nine in cotton-mills to twelve hours, but both these acts were ineffective as inspection was left to the magistrates and clergy. The first really effective act was the Factory Act of 1833, which applied to all textile factories, forbidding the employ-

18. Women workers at the looms in an early factory (*far right, top*).

19. In 1842 a government report was published on coal mining, which included this picture (*far right, centre*) and also Fig. 20. The report condemned the use of children chained to the coal wagons in narrow tunnels. Women and children were barred from working in mines by the Act of 1842. Notice the naked flame at the front of the wagon in this picture – despite the danger of explosion there was no Davy Lamp (Fig. 13) for this boy.

ment of children under nine and limiting the hours of those between nine and thirteen to nine a day and of those between thirteen and eighteen to twelve; and it provided for the appointment of government inspectors to see that the law was obeyed.

For the reformers this was just a beginning, and it was followed by others in the nineteenth century. The age at which children might begin work in any factory was reduced to ten by 1878. The Ten Hours Act of 1847 limited the working hours of all women and of boys under eighteen and benefited, in fact, men also because factories were not profitable if kept open for them alone. The fencing of dangerous machinery was ordered in 1844. And in 1867 the Factories and Workshops Act defined a factory as any place employing more than five people. This meant, therefore, that throughout industry the workpeople were protected by the law, and government inspectors could see that they did not suffer from bad conditions of employment.

Background
1 Look at Fig. 19, which shows a young boy working in a coal mine. Find out what sort of diseases these children suffered from. When were the conditions of child labour controlled by law?

Find out the diseases in general that resulted from work in factories and mines. For a start, imagine what happens when you work in a very dirty place: with very poor light; or where you cannot stand up straight.
2 Find out what sort of laws control factory work today. What arrangements does the government make to see that these laws are carried out?
3 Which natural resources (iron, coal, oil, gas etc.) does Britain produce herself and which does she import? Find out which other countries have enough of these resources for their own use.

20. The government report caption to this coal-mining picture (*left*) read: 'Ambler and Dyson being drawn up together, cross-lapped on the clatch iron. As soon as they arrived at the top, the handle was made fast by a bolt drawn from the upright post, and the woman then grasped the hands of both at the same time and by main force brought them to land.'

15

7 Transport and Communications

The Industrial Revolution could never have taken place in Britain without improvements in transport. Until about 1750 the best way to send goods was by ships along the coast. This was because the roads were too bad for long journeys to be undertaken by wheeled vehicles. In every parish all the able-bodied men were supposed to work six days a year on repairing the roads, but it was difficult to get them to do this. Travellers in coaches were commonly overturned by huge ruts or stuck in stretches of mud. In the eighteenth century, however, groups of men were allowed to take over lengths of road and erect gates or turnpikes at which they charged tolls to travellers in return for maintaining the road. It was possible for them to improve the roads because of the work of a number of great highway engineers, among whom was John Macadam, the inventor of a new road surface, composed of a tight mixture of broken stones, sand and water, which is still called after him.

The improved turnpike roads brought in the great age of coaching. From about 1750 stage coaches, which changed horses at fixed stages (usually inns), began to run between large towns. While it had previously taken three weeks to travel the four hundred miles from Edinburgh to London, now a coach took between ten and twelve days. And in 1784 the Post Office began to use specially designed coaches which carried both passengers and the mail at still faster speeds.

Industry, however, did not benefit much from the better roads because bulky goods could still not be sent on them. To meet this need, canals were dug at about the same time as the improvement of the roads. Within a few years Britain had thousands of miles of canals, mostly in the North and the Midlands (Fig. 21) to serve the new factory towns. They brought industry the coal and raw materials it needed, transported the manufactured goods from the factories to the ports and brought food for the workers. It was cheap to carry large loads on the canals, but it was also slow. The average speed of a barge on a canal was two-and-a-half miles an hour.

It was natural, therefore, men to consider whether steam-power could be adopted for transport. At first the early, heavy steam-engines were used to propel boats. In 1803 a Scottish engineer, William Symington, ran the first steam-boat, the *Charlotte Dundas*, on the Forth and Clyde Canal. Once he had shown it could be done, more and even larger steamships were built. By 1837 steamships were sailing to America and India. They were all paddleships and carried sails as well as engines which they often used only on calm days, but as the century progressed steam-power steadily displaced sail on the seas.

Steam carriages (Fig. 23), designed to travel on the roads, were made by several men, but the future lay with the railway system. Since the seventeenth century rails had been laid down in northern England to enable the horses, taking the coal in trucks from the mines to the river-quays, to pull heavier loads. In 1815 George Stephenson, a fireman in charge of a colliery pumping-engine, built a steam locomotive to travel on the rails. This was the beginning of a great revolution in transport. He built locomotives for the Stockton-Darlington (1825) and the Liverpool-Manchester (1830) lines, the first to be built in Britain; and he was the pioneer of many engineers who by the middle of the century had given the country a system of main lines linking the most important towns. For cheapness, speed and efficiency the railway was a means of transporting both passengers and goods beyond anything hitherto known.

The railways were assisted by another invention, the telegraph. In 1836, an American, Samuel Morse, devised the dot-and-dash telegraph system still called after him. A telegraph line was laid down between the signal boxes on the railway between Paddington and Slough in 1843, and it made news when it led to the arrest of a murderer who tried to escape to London by train. People now realized with wonder that messages could be sent instantly along wires for many hundreds of miles. Transport and communication were both overcoming the obstacle of space.

Background
1 Find out the history of any canal in your own area. What was it mainly used for? You could also find out when your local railways were built and what company ran them.
2 Demonstrate with diagrams how a boat is taken through a canal lock. Find out from British Waterways, the government department that runs the canals, how many canals are still in use.

21. British canals (*map, below left*).

22. An early steam-engine, the *Planet*.

23. A steam carriage, the *Obeissante*, in 1872 (*below*).

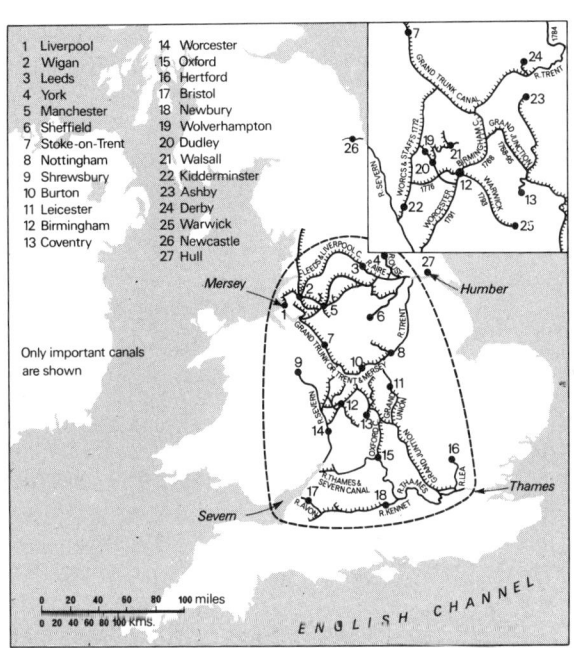

1 Liverpool	14 Worcester
2 Wigan	15 Oxford
3 Leeds	16 Hertford
4 York	17 Bristol
5 Manchester	18 Newbury
6 Sheffield	19 Wolverhampton
7 Stoke-on-Trent	20 Dudley
8 Nottingham	21 Walsall
9 Shrewsbury	22 Kidderminster
10 Burton	23 Ashby
11 Leicester	24 Derby
12 Birmingham	25 Warwick
13 Coventry	26 Newcastle
	27 Hull

Only important canals are shown

Mersey

Humber

Severn

Thames

0 20 40 60 80 100 miles
0 20 40 60 80 100 Kms.

ENGLISH CHANNEL

8 Capitalism

The more the Industrial Revolution developed, the more money was needed by manufacturers to carry on their business. Under the old domestic system, the clothier who supervized the production of cloth probably owned the yarn which he distributed to the weavers in their cottages and perhaps also the looms which they used, but the money he had to spend on these was not much. It was different, however, with the rise of factories employing hundreds of workers and using machines driven at first by water-power and then by steam-power. Manufacturers then had to get vast sums of money to buy the land, buildings, equipment and machinery needed to produce the goods they wanted to make.

In the beginning it was possible for a group of comparatively few men to supply the money or capital needed by an industrial enterprise. The usual arrangement in those early days of the Industrial Revolution was for two or three men to combine as partners, who invested their money in their undertaking and exercised control over it. The partnership of James Watt and Matthew Boulton to manufacture the steam-engine was an example of such an arrangement, while Richard Arkwright, after he had invented the water-frame, entered into partnership with two merchant employers in the hosiery trade, who in 1771 built a cotton-mill at Cromford on the River Derwent, which by 1779 was giving employment to 300 workers and was one of the first factories of the new age.

Besides such 'fixed capital', the manufacturers also needed 'circulating capital' to buy raw materials, to pay wages and to keep their factories and workshops in running order. To supply them with this, country banks or 'land banks' began operating in various parts of the country, lending them sums of money usually for short periods. Often this money came from landowners and farmers, being the profits they had made on the sale of their crops at the end of the harvest on which they were glad to gain interest until they needed it to buy seed and equipment the next year.

As an industry expanded, however, it required ever more capital, especially 'fixed capital'. At first the money required for extensions to factories and other needs was found by the original partners putting back their profits into the business or taking on additional partners; but the time came when this was not enough. In 1759, for instance, another inventor, John Roebuck, joined with a few partners, including his three brothers, to set up the Carron Iron-works in Stirlingshire, which before the end of the century had become the greatest munition works in Europe. Before then its capital had risen from £12,000 in 1760 to £150,000 in 1771, and the story was the same in other undertakings. If industry were not to be crippled by lack of

24. Some capitalists tried seriously to build model villages around their factories. Two of the most famous of these were Robert Owen (New Lanark Mills) and George Cadbury (Bournville, Birmingham). Another was Sir Titus Salt. Fig. 24 shows his model village and factory, called Saltaire, near Bradford. The houses had proper drainage, the village had public parks and proper hospitals and schools. It took twenty years to build.

capital, money had to be raised in some other way.

An alternative arrangement to a partnership is the joint-stock company in which control is separated from ownership. The company is managed by directors, who are paid salaries, while a much larger body of people own the capital, which is divided into shares which may be bought and sold freely. The shareholders get a regular dividend paid from the profits of the company on each share. Until the middle of the nineteenth century, however, joint-stock companies suffered from a number of disadvantages, the most serious being that if a company went bankrupt, all the shareholders were liable for its debts and might have their private property seized to pay them. This was finally remedied by the Limited Liability Act of 1855 which empowered joint-stock companies to limit the liability of their shareholders to the shares they owned. If such companies fail, the shareholders lose their shares, but do not suffer further loss. Companies of this sort are recognizable by the word 'Limited' or 'Ltd.' after their name.

Such protection from the law enabled the joint-stock company to become the normal way of raising capital, and through it the railways and the rest of Britain's great enterprises were made possible. Shares in joint-stock companies are bought and sold through stockbrokers at the stock exchanges, the most important one in Britain being the Stock Exchange in London. The price of shares depends upon a number of factors, such as the profits made by a company and its prospects for the future, and this is important for investors to know since fortunes can be made or lost by buying and selling shares.

This system by which industry is organized and financed is known as capitalism. Stockholders are of all sorts. Some hold only a few shares in which they have invested their savings; some hold many shares, and among the wealthiest are insurance companies, pension funds and other bodies which need a steady income. All, however, have one thing in common. They have lent their money to the companies in the expectation of getting a profit from it, and the success of a company is judged by its ability to do this.

Background

1 Find out about the Stock Exchange 'crash' of 1929. What happened in America's stock exchange (Wall Street, New York) and in London? How did this affect the working people?
2 What industries are now run by the government that used to be run by private owners? When were they taken over?

25. The Stock Exchange.

9 Britain's World Trade

'It would not be worth my while', said Matthew Boulton, speaking of his steam engines, 'to make for three counties only; but I find it worth my while to make for the world'. When he spoke Britain, because of the advance in industrialization she had obtained over all other countries, was known as the 'Workshop of the World'. If British manufacturers had been able to sell their goods in Britain alone, her Industrial Revolution would inevitably have been a comparatively small movement, but no other country in those days could rival her as supplier of the industrial products they needed if they were to take advantage of the developments of the new age.

The result was that British overseas trade grew at an ever-increasing rate during the eighteenth and nineteenth centuries. British exports, for instance, doubled between 1700 and 1763, but they increased nearly fivefold between 1848 and 1872. In the opening years of the nineteenth century, by far the most important of Britain's exports were manufactured articles of cotton, which were sold not only in Europe but in the tropical countries as well. Other exports included wool, linen and silk, hardware, cutlery and leather goods.

As the century progressed, cotton goods continued to hold their lead as exports, but they were joined by other important industrial products. Iron exports grew with astonishing rapidity because it was needed for girders, bridges, railway lines and many other engineering works which other countries were now taking in hand. Coal exports also increased steadily as steam power was adopted for industry and transport in all parts of the world. The development of the railways alone stimulated British trade. In many countries they were designed by British engineers, used rolling-stock made on Tyneside, ran on rails manufactured in Glasgow and burnt coal mined in South Wales.

Britain was fortunate in having her own

26. The opening of the Suez Canal in 1869 (*below*). The narrow path of land left for the ceremony was cut through to join the Mediterranean to the Red Sea. Is the canal as important today as it was then?

27. British industrial production seen as a percentage of world production, 1750–1958 (*below right*). See also Fig. 31.

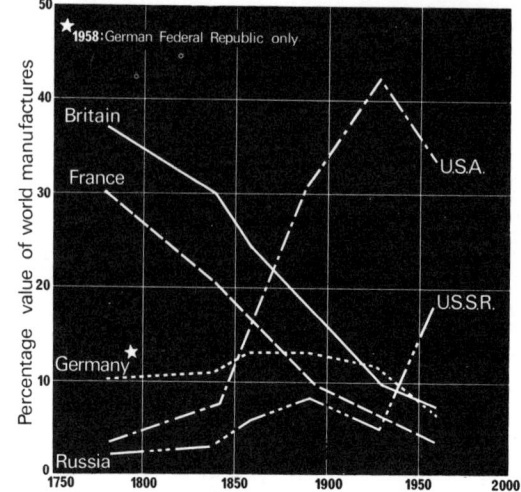

natural resources of coal and iron, but she had to import other raw materials needed by her industry such as cotton, jute, timber and tin. Increasingly she had also to import another commodity – food. Quite early in the nineteenth century her population grew beyond the level at which it could be fed by her own agriculture. By the middle of the century nearly a quarter of her bread was made from wheat grown abroad. At first British farming was protected by the Corn Laws, which levied a duty on imports of foreign wheat, but in 1846 these laws were repealed. By then, duties on raw materials and nearly all other imports had been removed, so that Britain became a free trade country at the same time as she had developed into an industrial state, compelled to buy and sell in the world to maintain her people.

To carry on this trade, she needed ports and shipping. In the century between 1750 and 1850 both Liverpool and Glasgow grew more than twelve times in size and, together with London, became among the greatest ports in the world. The British mercantile marine also increased so

that by the end of the nineteenth century nearly half the world's shipping tonnage flew the British flag. The opening of the Suez Canal in 1869 (Fig. 26) greatly assisted British trade, and so did the oceanic telegraph cables which were laid in the third quarter of the century.

Britain had become so wealthy by the middle of the century that she was able to export capital as well as goods. Her money went to pay for the construction of railways, the digging of mines and the equipment of factories in many countries. The interest earned by this capital, together with the profits of her shipping, became 'invisible exports' which helped to pay for her imports of food and raw materials. Through trade the standard of living enjoyed by her people rose. Food became more plentiful, clothing cheaper and housing better.

Background

1 Britain was a great exporter of machinery. What sort of advantage did this give the countries in Fig. 27. Which countries now export machinery?

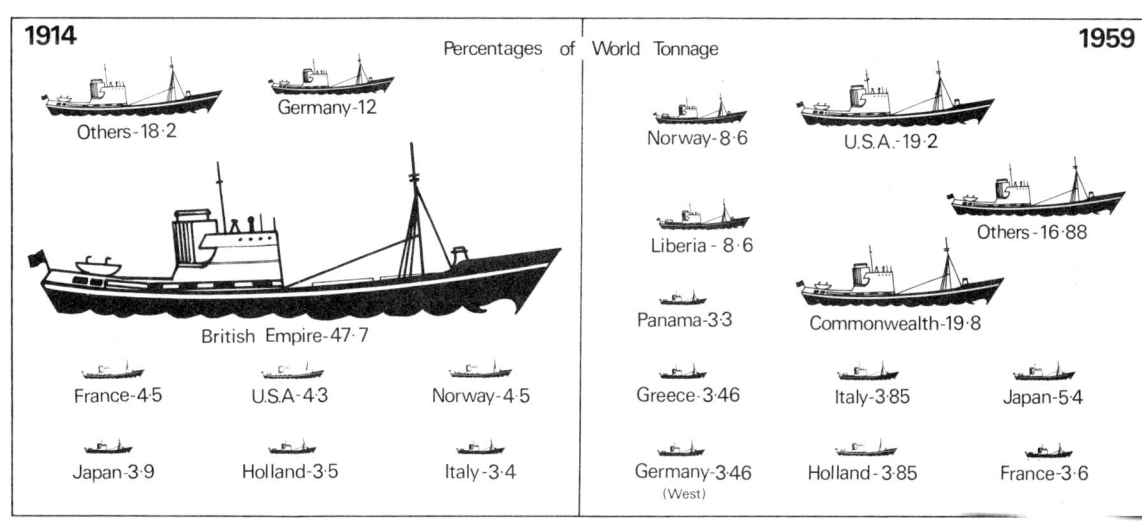

1914   Percentages of World Tonnage   1959

Others - 18·2   Germany - 12

British Empire - 47·7

France - 4·5   U.S.A. - 4·3   Norway - 4·5

Japan - 3·9   Holland - 3·5   Italy - 3·4

Norway - 8·6   U.S.A. - 19·2

Liberia - 8·6   Others - 16·88

Panama - 3·3   Commonwealth - 19·8

Greece - 3·46   Italy - 3·85   Japan - 5·4

Germany - 3·46 (West)   Holland - 3·85   France - 3·6

28. The diagrams show percentages of the tonnage of the world's shipping in 1914 and 1959. Why do small countries like Liberia and Panama have such a large share of modern shipping?

10 The Continuation of the Revolution

Once the Industrial Revolution had begun to change the life and work of many people, its progress continued unchecked. The success of new changes and discoveries stimulated inventors to seek out yet more improvements, while the growing demand for the products of industry meant that manufacturers were ready to adopt fresh ways of increasing the output of their factories. A consequence of this was that industry was more ready to bring into use the achievements of the scientists. The time-lag between scientific invention and discovery and their application to industry became steadily less during the nineteenth century.

Since the need for iron became greater than ever, improvements in its production were particularly sought, and two important changes were made in the first half of the century. In 1829 James Neilson of Glasgow invented the hot-blast furnace, which greatly reduced fuel consumption by using a blast of hot instead of cold air and so avoiding the loss of heat in the furnace.

29. James Nasmyth's steam hammer, 1839.

And in 1839 James Nasmyth invented a steam-hammer which was of great use in forging iron. Iron output rose from a million tons in 1833 to three million in 1855 and to six million in 1865. There was a particularly urgent need for improvements in the production of steel (which is iron combined with carbon to make it harder). For centuries Sheffield had made excellent steel, but the process was so long and costly that it could only be used for springs and cutting implements. In 1856, however, Henry Bessemer divised a converter in which the impurities were removed from the iron by a blast of hot air and the right amount of carbon added afterwards. The price of steel soon fell from £40 to £5 a ton, and in 1867 William Siemans invented a gas 'open-hearth' furnace which made it still cheaper. Neither of these processes, however, eliminated phosphorous which was found in most iron ores. This difficulty was overcome in 1879 by the Gilchrist-Thomas process, invented by two English chemists, in which the converter was lined with lime-stone to absorb the phosphorous. These three inventions meant that steel replaced iron in the manufacture of ships, locomotives, railway lines, bridges and all sorts of machinery.

The first large all-steel ship to be built was the Cunard liner *Servia*, which went into service in 1881. And one of the first uses of the turbine was to drive steamships with greater speed and power. Indeed, Sir Charles Parsons demonstrated the superiority of his invention by fitting one into a small boat, the *Turbinia*, which sped between the warships at Queen Victoria's Diamond Jubilee Review at Spithead in 1897 so rapidly that no naval vessel could catch it.

From the early years of the twentieth century its use became common in ships, and at the same time the adaptation of ships to oil-burning saved time and man-power and brought cleanliness compared with the coal-burning ships.

Other important developments were concerned with the preservation of food. The food-canning industry began about 1875, but more important for Britain (with her need to import food from abroad) was the invention of refrigeration. In 1882 the steamship *Dunedin* brought the first load of frozen New Zealand mutton to London. The method was soon extended to Australian mutton, Argentinian beef, and butter, cheese, poultry and fruit from several distant countries. It was now possible to satisfy the demands of the prosperous British people for a more abundant and varied diet.

Before the end of the century, several inventions had been made which were to be of immense importance in the future. Michael Faraday had discovered in 1831 electro-magnetic induction, which led to the making of practical dynamos in the 1870s, while in 1878 Joseph Swan invented the filament electric lamp. Electric-lighting began to replace coal gas-lighting (first used in London in 1814) before the end of the century, but electric power was only slowly used. Similarly, Gottlieb Daimler had developed the internal combustion engine in 1885, but the threat of the motor car to the railway as the supreme means of transport had yet to be made.

Background

1 Find out how a Bessemer converter works. Compare it to what you can find out about a modern blast furnace.

2 Make a list of the foodstuffs in your own home. Where does each one come from? How many of them need refrigeration to keep them fresh?

30. Making steel by the Bessemer process. On the right the air blast is going through the converter. The converter on the left is being loaded and in the centre molten steel is being poured into moulds to form ingots.

11 The Challenge from Overseas

By about 1870 the trade of Britain with overseas countries had about reached its zenith. At that time it largely exceeded the trade of France, Germany and Italy put together; and if the trade of the British colonies were added to it, then that of the United States of America could be placed on the other side, and still the combination would be beaten. Moreover, this comparison, astonishing as it is, does not reveal the whole situation; for while the export trade of these other countries was as yet almost entirely in food and raw materials, much of which (such as American wheat and cotton) was sold to Britain, the great bulk of British exports continued to be in manufactured goods.

During the last quarter of the nineteenth century, however, the situation steadily changed to Britain's disadvantage. Other countries began to challenge her position by establishing industries of their own which they protected against competition from British industry by setting up tariffs against her goods. One country after another placed heavy duties upon the products which Britain wished to sell to their people –

Germany in 1879, France in 1882 and the United States in 1890. Even the British dominions did the same; Canada adopted high tariffs in 1879 and so did the Commonwealth of Australia as soon as it was formed in 1900. Britain meanwhile remained a free-trade country and was not to adopt a system of tariffs until 1932.

Behind the shield of these tariffs, such countries were able to build up new industries which were more up-to-date than their older British counterparts. Two countries in particular mounted a formidable challenge to Britain. America overtook her as a steel proceducer in 1890 and by 1913 had an output four times as great; Germany overtook her in 1893 and by 1913 had an output more than twice as great. Strangely enough, Britain herself assisted the rise of these rival industrial nations. Foreigners, who were starting new factories behind tariff walls, needed machines to equip them, and up to 1900 they bought them chiefly from Britain. So, while in the mid-Victorian period British exports had consisted mainly of manufactured articles, the sale of these now began to decline,

31. Britain's share of world industry in the nineteenth century. See also Fig. 27.

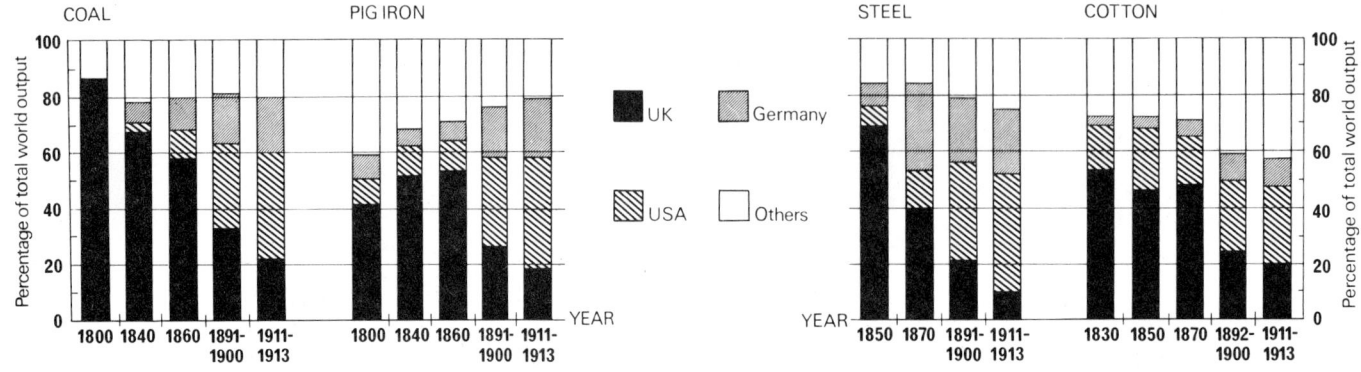

and she began to sell machines (which equipped foreigners to do without her manufactures) and ships (which enabled foreigners to cease using her shipping). While they lasted, such exports were valuable for Britain, and no doubt others would have supplied them if she did not, but it hastened the loss of her position as the 'Workshop of the World'.

There were other reasons for this decline. British industry began to suffer from the fact that it had been the first in the world. Factories and machines were becoming out-of-date, and industrialists had done so well in the past that they saw no need for change or improvement. British inventors often found they could get more recognition abroad. For instance, Graham Bell, a Scotsman, went to America where he invented the telephone in 1875. Furthermore, while previously most of the important new inventions and developments had taken place in Britain, now they were increasingly originating in other countries. The new electrical and chemical industries and the manufacture of the motor-car were pioneered elsewhere. Britain had lost her 'industrial leadership'.

The main reason, however, for Britain's changed position lay in her size and resources. Though Britain's population had increased so considerably since the eighteenth century, she still remained a small island. A number of circumstances had made her the world's first industrial nation and given her an advantage over all other nations, both large and small; but there were other nations with larger populations, territories and resources. When they became industrialized, they could outpace Britain, and when oil and electricity began to replace coal and steam-power in the twentieth century, she was at a further disadvantage. She was now a small, thickly-populated country, compelled to buy food for her people by selling her manufactures in competition with the great industrial nations of the world.

Background
1 Where does Britain stand in relation to Germany and America in industrial power today? Find out too about Japan's industrial revolution.
2 What are the main areas of competition between British and other countries' industries? List the main British Companies making, for example, cars, electrical goods, textiles or chemicals, and put opposite them their main overseas rivals.

32. Britain's share of steel production, 1948–1960 (*centre*). Figures for the output of steel are in millions of metric tons.

33. Britain's share of motor vehicle production, 1948–1960 (*bottom*). Figures for vehicle production are in millions.

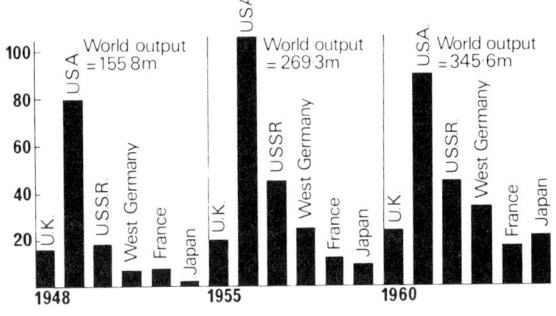

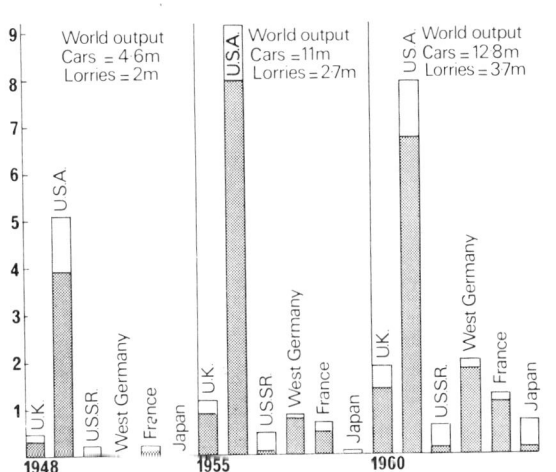

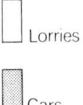

25

12 Socialism

Capitalism made Britain's industrial development possible, and it brought riches to industrialists and investors, but it also brought into being a large working-class who possessed no property and were entirely dependent upon their low, hard-earned wages. Such an unequal distribution of wealth caused the workers to form trade unions in which they united in efforts to improve their wages and working conditions. It also led some reformers to urge that property and industry should in some way be held for the good of all. An early upholder of this idea, which came to be known as socialism, was Robert Owen who in 1799 organized the New Lanark Mills in Scotland as a model factory with good pay and working conditions, houses and medical

care for the workers and schools for their children. He believed that the profits of industry should be devoted to the benefit of the workers, though he did not consider that they should have any share in its management.

The man who did most to make socialism a force capable of rivalling capitalism was Karl Marx, a German Jew who from 1849 until his death in 1883 lived in exile and poverty in London. He studied and wrote in the reading room of the British Museum, having previously published the *Communist Manifesto*, which ended with the call, 'Workers of the world, unite!' Marx stated that capitalism exploited the workers, whose labour produced a greater value than the wages they received, and he called upon the workers everywhere to realize their wrongs and their strength, to seize power and replace capitalism by a new socialist (or communist) society in which there would be public ownership of all means of production, the elimination of all social classes and the realization of the principle of 'from each according to his capacities, to each according to his needs'. He proclaimed the necessity for an uprising of the workers to bring about a revolution in which the existing order would be overthrown and a 'dictatorship of the working-classes' established.

In the later part of the nineteenth century, socialist or communist parties were established in a number of countries, but when the revolution came, it did not break out (as Marx had thought it would) in one of the advanced industrial countries. It broke out in Russia which was backward and hardly-industrialized and on the verge of defeat by Germany in the First World War. The chaos and suffering in the war-torn country enabled the Russian Communists to seize power in 1917 and proclaim Russia as the 'first socialist state in the world'. Such socialism made the government all-powerful since it controlled all the country's industry, and it set out to make Russia a modern manufacturing state. Factories, mines and hydro-electric works were built. Towards the end of the 1930s coal production had increased fivefold and steel production sixfold. Russia had become one of the world's great industrial powers.

In Britain Marx's ideas were slow in gaining acceptance among the working classes. When he came to London there were British trade unions, but they were confined largely to skilled craftsmen such as engineers, carpenters, bricklayers and printers, and they were non-revolutionary bodies, which accepted the prevailing organization of industry and sought to improve the position of their members by individual negotiations and agreements with the employers. In 1868, however, these unions formed the Trade Union Congress to enable them to take united action, and gradually trade unions were formed among other workers. In the later part of the nineteenth century foreign competition produced severe industrial depression in Britain in which the non-skilled workers suffered most. They adopted demonstrations and strikes as a means of improving their pay and conditions, but the revolutionary ideal, proclaimed by Marx, won little acceptance. Instead, the Trade Union Congress in 1906 established the Labour party to forward its aims in politics, and in 1918 it declared itself in favour of a policy of socialism. It aimed, however, at achieving this, not by violence, but by winning popular support by democratic means.

Not until 1945 did the Labour party secure an absolute majority in Parliament which enabled it to wield political power. It then nationalized the coal mines, the railways, the airways and the gas, electricity and steel industries. These have disappeared from the Stock Exchange, but a large part of British industry still remains under the control of joint-stock companies, some of which have now become very large. Britain has a mixed economy, a mixture of capitalism and socialism, which places it halfway between socialist Russia and capitalist America.

34. Unemployed Dockers in 1886 outside London's West India Docks (*far left*). The slogan reads 'Wanted, Wanted, Wanted, Rioters, Rioters. 100,000 Rioters Wanted for the West End to break and Smash all the Windows'.

35. Strike pickets argue with 'blackleg' workers outside a factory, 1969.

Background

1 The traditional weapon of the workers has been the strike. Find out about the General Strike of 1926. What other ways can workers use to influence the management?

2 How do strikers live while they are on strike? How much money do they contribute to their Union and what do they get in return? Make a questionnaire and put questions like this to Trade Union members that you know.

13 The Culmination of the Revolution

The great achievement of the Industrial Revolution was to put into effect the idea of mechanization by getting machines to assist the work of several hundred men all assembled together in a single factory instead of having each man doing his own task separately in his own home or workshop through his own muscle power. This was made possible by the use of the steam-engine with coal as its fuel.

Mechanization still remains the essential way in which industry is organized to-day, but the source of power employed is changing. In many modern factories, instead of a great steam-engine driving all the machines by a system of belts and pulleys from a single shaft, each machine has its own electric motor designed to give it the speed and power it needs. Some of the power stations which provide electricity for these machines use coal to create steam to drive their dynamos, and some use oil, but Calder Hall has been followed by other nuclear power stations; and though these are still more expensive to operate than the older power stations, they already provide about a fifth of the electricity used in Britain, and this amount is likely to go on increasing. At the same time, the discovery of large reserves of natural gas beneath the North Sea promises to provide a relatively cheap source of power.

The development of these new sources of power have badly hit the coal industry, without which the Industrial Revolution could never have taken place. Other old-established basic industries have also suffered. Iron and steel have met competition from plastics and new metals like aluminium; cotton has been displaced by nylon, rayon and other synthetic fibres; and shipping has had to meet the steady growth of air travel. Consequently coal-mines, cotton-mills and shipyards have been forced to close down in large numbers. Tyneside and Lancashire, Clydeside and South Wales, the once-prosperous areas of the country, have had to endure unemployment and distress.

In place of the old heavy industries, new light industries are arising. Factories are now making chemicals for industrial explosives, fertilizers and medicines; new processed foods; ready-to-wear clothes; and manufactured goods such as washing-machines and vacuum cleaners, radio and television sets, motor cars and aeroplanes. These new factories are very different from the old. They do not have to be situated near the coal and iron fields. Southern England and the Midlands have become increasingly important as manufacturing regions, but industrialization has not made them like the older areas. As a

36. Britain's nuclear power stations for generating electricity.

writer has said, the typical new factory 'is not a gaunt barrack or an awful chaos of blackness and belching chimneys; it is a glittering white structure of concrete, glass and steel, surrounded by green lawns and beds of tulips' (Orwell).

These are new turns taken by the Industrial Revolution, but the change which represents its highest and final phase is the mass-production of manufactured articles. This was well established by 1850, especially for firearms and clocks, and in 1909 Henry Ford began to make cheap motor cars in America in this way. He arranged his factory so that each workman fitted one small part of a car in place as it passed him on a moving assembly belt. When the car reached the end of the factory, it could be driven off and tested. Nowadays all sorts of goods are made in this way.

This process, like the earlier developments of the Industrial Revolution, has eliminated the use of the worker's muscles, but continued to rely on his brain. Thus, there are two main stages in making motor cars – constructing the parts of the cars and assembling these parts to form the cars. Though both have been highly mechanized, each still demands some human thought. The men working at the drilling and milling machines have to think about putting the pieces of metal into the correct place before the machines can actually start making the car parts; and on the assembly lines the men and women have to give some thought about which screw to turn and which bolt to tighten. But now this is changing.

37. An aerial view of the Bradwell nuclear power station.

14 Another Industrial Revolution

So far this book has been about the Industrial Revolution, but it is called *Industrial Evolution* because it now seems that the Industrial Revolution, which has made so many changes in our lives, is giving place to an another, equally revolutionary movement. This new Industrial Revolution is based upon computers. These machines are like electric brains which can record information, solve problems and control other machines. They have given us the fresh process of 'automation'.

So now it is possible to run a motor-car works or any other mass-production factory in an entirely different way. In the first stage of producing, for instance, a new motor car or aircraft, the designer at his desk translates his drawing into a list of instructions in the form of algebraic expressions about the lines and curves he wants the milling machine to make. A girl then types these instructions as a code on a strip of paper like a ticker-tape from a teleprinter. This strip is fed into a computer that does the sums, working out the curves and lines of which it has been given the algebraic formula, and issues the answers as a length of magnetic tape. This tape is put into the automatic controller of the milling machine, and the machine then gets to work manufacturing the part it has been instructed to produce. To make another part, exactly the same as the first, the magnetic tape is simply put through the control gear again. An expensive milling machine can be kept operating continually because its control is performed automatically. Similarly, an expensive computer, when it has finished working out the sums needed to produce a tape to instruct one milling machine how to make a particular shape, can then be set to work out the calculations required for other tapes to produce other shapes by a series of other machines that may be either in the

38. The assembly line at a major car factory. As the car bodies go past, each man completes one part of the process.

same factory or in other factories that have sent in drawings.

In the same way, the manufacturing operations in a factory can be done completely automatically. Great transfer machines can automatically move metal pieces from one part to another of a factory until the whole series of operations has been completed. And in the assembly stage, a computer can watch over the components travelling along the several diverse assembly lines, so that a complete finished article (or at least a large part of one) can be put together without anyone having to think about it. Already in pea-canning factories the entire process – selecting and cooking the peas, fashioning, filling and sealing the cans – is done entirely atuomatically from start to finish, and there is no doubt that this method will spread to other sorts of factories.

Nor are computers revolutionizing only the manufacturing side of industry. They are likely to make as thorough changes in the management side as well. A computer can report on the monthly production from a number of

39. Automatic 'robotugs' move goods in a warehouse (*above left*) directed by one man at a control panel (*above right*).

40. Inside one of the world's largest computer centres (*left*) at Cape Kennedy, space flight co-ordinators turn away from the control panels to watch the TV monitors.

factories a few days after the end of the month and can examine the output and effectiveness of different departments and machines. And when the goods pass from the factories to the shops, computers will enable the headquarters of a large firm to keep account of every article sold in its branches, to have it automatically replaced and to note the daily trend of sales.

The first Industrial Revolution brought about the mechanization of muscle power through coal; this new Industrial Revolution will bring about the mechanization of brainpower through electronics. One effect it will certainly have. It will drastically reduce the amount of time that men and women will have to spend at their paid employment. An expert has recently forecast that industry's present labour force will be reduced by a half by the mid-1980s because of the effects of computers. Already there are industries in which a four-day week is accepted. Next will doubtless come a three-day week, which might be turned into a six-month year or perhaps people might prefer to work a $23\frac{1}{2}$ year lifetime and retire on full pay at the age of 41. At any rate, people in the future are likely to have much more leisure. What are they going to do with it?

Background

1 Try to find examples of industries where men have lost their jobs because of automation. Compare these to industries where automation has created more demand and thus the need for more trained men to use the new machines.

2 Make a survey of leisure in your own area. How many cinemas, theatres, dance-halls, sports grounds etc. have you got? Are they fully used? Would they be used more if people had more time? Are there minority recreations that are not well provided for?

THOMAS NELSON AND SONS LTD
36 Park Street London W1Y 4DE
P.O. Box 18123 Nairobi Kenya

THOMAS NELSON (AUSTRALIA) LTD
597 Little Collins Street Melbourne 3000

THOMAS NELSON AND SONS (CANADA) LTD
81 Curlew Drive Don Mills Ontario

THOMAS NELSON (NIGERIA) LTD
P.O. Box 336 Apapa Lagos

THOMAS NELSON AND SONS (SOUTH AFRICA) (PROPRIETARY) LTD
51 Commissioner Street Johannesburg

ISBN 0 17 435001 5

Printed offset in Great Britain by
The Camelot Press Ltd, London and Southampton

Acknowledgements are due to the following for permission to reproduce illustrations:

The Mansell Collection (3, 5, 9, 10–15, 17–20, 22–24, 26, 34);

Aerofilms Ltd (6);

The Science Museum (16);

The Keystone Press Agency Ltd (25, 35);

Mary Evans Picture Library (29, 30);

Central Electricity Generating Board (37);

Ford Motor Company (U.K.) Ltd (38);

H. J. Heinz Co Ltd (39);

International Business Machines Ltd (40);

The Economist (7);

Front cover picture of Charcoal Burning (1750) by courtesy of the Mansell Collection.

Back cover picture of the digital computer controlling the Saturn rocket launches by courtesy of I.B.M. (U.K.) Ltd.

Design by Michael Lloyd.